HAL LEONARD
GUITAR METHOD

COUNTRY GUITAR

BY GREG KOCH

W9-BLC-596

ISBN 978-0-634-03949-2

HAL•LEONARD®
CORPORATION
7777 W. BLUEMOUND RD. P.O. BOX 13819 MILWAUKEE, WI 53213

Visit Hal Leonard Online at
www.halleonard.com

CONTENTS

	PAGE	TRACK
Introduction	4	
Acoustic or Electric?	4	
Picking	5	
Standing vs. Sitting	5	
Cowboy Chords	6	
Tuning Notes	6	1
Sweet Dreams	6	2
Rocky Top	7	3
Scales and Chords	8	
C Major Scale	8	4
Chords in C	9	
Improvising in C	10	5-10
Carter Picking	11	
I Walk the Line	11	11
The Hammer-On	12	12
The Pull-Off	12	13
Wildwood Flower	13	14
"Boom Chick" Rhythm	14	
Hey, Good Lookin' (Rhythm)	14	15
The Slide	16	16
The Major Pentatonic	16	17-19
Hey, Good Lookin' (Melody)	17	20
The String Bend	18	21
Vibrato	18	22
Chattahoochie	18	23
G Major	20	24-25
Barre Chords	21	
A-Type Barre Chord	21	
Ramblin' Man (Chorus)	22	26
Hammer-On Rhythm Exercise (in G)	22	27
Double Stops in Thirds	23	28
Ring of Fire	24	29
G Major Pentatonic with Added ♭3rd	26	30-32
Sugarfoot Rag	27	33-34
D Major	28	
Licks	29	35-37
Chords	29	

	PAGE	TRACK
E-Type Barre Chord	30	
Mercury Blues	31	38
I–vi–IV–V	31	39
Sus Chords & Seventh Chords	32	
Dsus Waltz	33	40
Buckaroo	34	41
Grace Notes	36	42
Forever and Ever, Amen	36	43, 46
D Major Pentatonic w/Added ♭3rd	38	44-45
A Major	39	47-48
Travis Picking	40	49-50
Pickin' in A	40	51
Freight Train	41	52
Movable Scales	42	
Major	42	53-54
Major Pentatonic with Added ♭3rd	43	55-56
Chicken Pickin'	44	57-59
Country Gentleman	45	60-61
Twelve-Bar Blues	48	
The Shuffle Rhythm	48	62-64
Move It On Over	49	65, 70
The Blues Scale	50	66-69
Sixteen Tons	51	71
Movable Shuffle Patterns	52	72-73
The Race Is On	52	74, 81
Extending and Blending Scales	54	75-80
Riffs and Licks in E	56	
James Burton's "Susie-Q" Riff	56	82
Mystery Train	56	83
Little Sister	56	84
Folsom Prison Blues (Intro)	57	85
Boogie Patterns	57	86
Hot Rod Lincoln (riff)	57	87
Blended Licks	58	88-91
Sixths	58	92-98
Rebel 'Rouser	60	99

INTRODUCTION

Welcome to the Hal Leonard Country Guitar method. The realm of what is considered "country guitar" has really evolved in the last few decades into one of the most exciting and challenging styles of guitar playing. Today, country guitar incorporates a broad range of influences, from traditional sounds like Travis picking, chicken pickin', bluegrass, and Western swing to the contemporary phrasing of modern blues and rock.

In this book, we'll touch on many different techniques using simplified yet authentic arrangements of country guitar classics. Working through tunes by everyone from Johnny Cash to fret-burner Albert Lee, you'll acquire the basic skills to "pick a few tunes" by yourself or "fire up a jam" with some friends.

ACOUSTIC OR ELECTRIC?

Most of the techniques in this book can be played on either acoustic or electric guitar. Some techniques may lend themselves more to acoustic guitar; other techniques—like string bending—will be easier on electric. Let's briefly talk about some classic acoustic and electric guitars that may help you in finding a country sound.

Any acoustic guitar can get you started, but here are a few things to consider. A guitar with a solid top—meaning that the face of the guitar is made of pieces of solid wood (most commonly spruce) instead of particle board or laminate—is going to give you a more resonant, superior tone. Some of the biggest names in top-quality acoustics most commonly found in the hands of country artists, both past and present, include Martin, Gibson, and Guild. The sizes of the instruments vary, but the "dreadnought" is the most popular and is available in a variety of prices from a host of manufacturers.

The most popular electric guitar in country music has long been the Fender Telecaster. Players such as Jimmy Bryant, Luther Perkins (guitarist for Johnny Cash), Buck Owens, Waylon Jennings, Merle Haggard, James Burton, Albert Lee, Vince Gill, and session giant Brent Mason (to name just a few) have all defined electric country guitar greatness with a "Tele" in their hands. From "mellow" to maximum "twang," the Telecaster and its common counterpart, the Fender Twin amplifier, comprise the quintessential country guitar combo. Other classic country tones have come from guitars such as the Gretsch 6120 (in the hands of Chet Atkins) and the Gibson Super 400 (used by Merle Travis). The Gibson Les Paul and other humbucker-equipped guitars with a rounder, fatter tone, have also certainly made their mark in the idiom of country music. Clearly, however, single-coil pickups with their glassy, twang-friendly tone are the most widely used in country music.

As for amps, the Fender Twin and other similar-styled amps—especially Peavey—with their ability to output clean tones at high volumes were, for years, the chosen amps of most players. With rock and blues having an ever-increasing influence on contemporary country, amps with built-in distortion, such as modern Fenders, Peavey, and MESA/Boogie, are more frequently used.

When picking out a guitar and/or amplifier, find something that is user-friendly and that you look forward to playing. You do not have to spend a fortune on equipment; choose gear that will be an effective inspiration for you to play.

Dreadnought acoustic

Fender Tele with Fender Twin amp

PICKING

We'll begin our studies using basic flatpicking—that is, playing with a standard (flat) pick, held between your thumb and index finger. Eventually, though, if you're serious about playing country music, you'll want to try some method of picking that also incorporates your fingers. Basically, you'll have two options:

Hybrid Picking: A flat pick in conjunction with the other fingers (particularly the middle and ring) is the most widely used right-hand technique by modern country guitarists. This "hybrid" approach helps facilitate a variety of techniques/style nuances like Travis picking, chicken pickin', and pedal-steel bends. A little bit of nail growth on the middle and ring fingers will help you to "pop" the string more. Try this technique by gradually introducing the other fingers to parts you now comfortably play using just a pick. As with any technique, the more you practice, the better you'll get.

Thumb & Fingers: Another option is to use a thumbpick, with the other three or four fingers as "partners in crime." This technique, first popularized by Chet Atkins and Merle Travis and then further developed by modern super-pickers Brent Mason and Scotty Anderson, allows for the greatest speed, flexibility, and accuracy. If you are already extremely comfortable with conventional picking, it can be somewhat difficult to "jump ship" to using a thumb pick. However, if you are just developing an approach, one listen to Chet or Brent will state a powerful case for "thumbin' it."

basic flatpicking

hybrid picking

thumb and fingers

STANDING VS. SITTING

To prepare yourself for eventually performing in public or in front of your friends, I encourage you to periodically stand when you practice. This doesn't mean you need to stand every time you grab the guitar, but once you've got a new lick under your fingers, put a strap on your guitar and get used to playing it while standing. The way you distribute your weight, how you approach the fretboard and the strings, and how you support the instrument will all make a big difference in how well you play when standing versus sitting.

And while you're at it, plug it in. In the same way that the difference between sitting and standing can feel like night and day, plugging in to an amp (and turning up to "10") can be an eye-opening experience if you've been practicing your electric unplugged all the while. String dampening, dynamics, and overall tone can be grossly misjudged if not amplified, so be sure you spend enough time plugged in if the electric guitar is your instrument of choice.

Now let's get started!

COWBOY CHORDS

Open chords—that is, chords with one or more open strings, usually played within the first few frets of the guitar—have a sound that often conjures up the image of a cowboy strummin' away on the prairie. These types of voicings are commonly referred to as "cowboy chords."

Strum along with the following two country classics to get the hang of switching between some "cowboy" chord shapes. Listen to the CD and follow the suggested strum patterns.

 TUNING NOTES

TRACK 1

This first country favorite was immortalized by the great Patsy Cline and etched forever in the minds of guitarists by Telecaster deity Roy Buchanan.

SWEET DREAMS

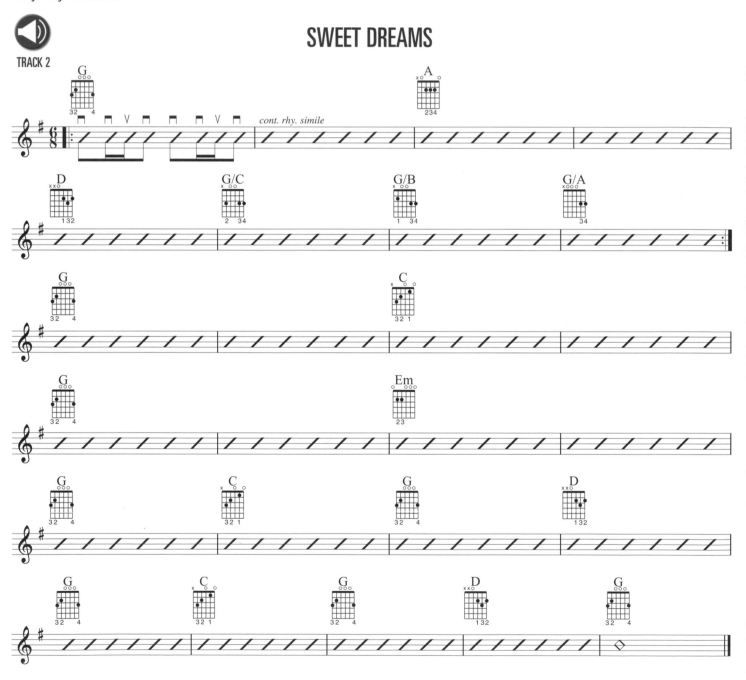

Your right hand will get quite a workout as you strum along to this second number, a well-known bluegrass tune. (If the pace is too fast for you, try two strums per measure instead of the pattern shown.)

ROCKY TOP

TRACK 3

SCALES AND CHORDS

A great way to combine a number of concepts that will develop your country guitar playing as well as your understanding of music in general is to study the major scales and the chords linked to them. Let's start with C major.

First of all, a **scale** is a series of notes arranged in a specific order. Perhaps the most common scale is the *major scale.* It is used as the basis for countless melodies, riffs, solos, and chord progressions.

Scales are constructed using a combination of whole steps and half steps. (On the guitar, a half step is the distance of one fret; a whole step is two frets.) All major scales are build from the following step pattern:

WHOLE–WHOLE–HALF–WHOLE–WHOLE–WHOLE–HALF

This series of whole and half steps gives the major scale its characteristic sound.

C MAJOR SCALE

To build a C major scale, start with the note C and follow the step pattern shown above.

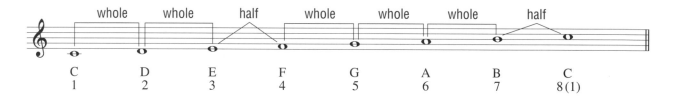

The first (and eighth) degree of a major scale is called the keynote or *tonic.* This is the "home" tone on which most melodies end.

Practice the C major scale, ascending and descending.

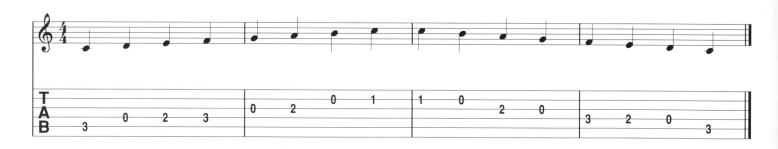

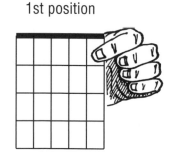
1st position

This scale is played in **first position**—that is, with your first finger at the first fret, second finger at the second fret, and so on. (The name of the position is determined by where you place your first finger.) We'll be learning a lot of scales and chords in this area of the fretboard—also called "open position"—as the combination of open and fretted notes available here tends to sound very "country" all by itself.

Try the following scale exercise. If you play it as indicated, using downstrokes (⊓) and upstrokes (∨)—i.e., **alternate picking**—you'll add to the "country" feel. Practice this slowly, without mistakes, and gradually speed it up as your technique allows.

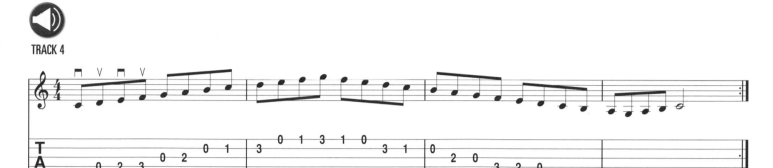

TRACK 4

CHORDS IN C

When a piece of music is based on a C major scale, it is said to be "in the key of" C. This could apply to a melody, licks, riffs, solos, and even to chords. For every key, there are seven corresponding chords—one built on each note of the scale.

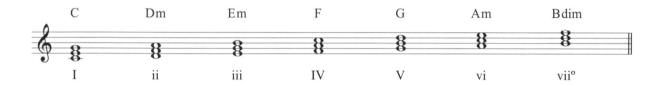

The seven chords are common to the key of C because all seven contain only notes of the C major scale (no sharps or flats). They're created by stacking notes in thirds—i.e., every other note of the scale (1-3-5, 2-4-6, etc.). Because each consists of three notes, these chords are also sometimes referred to as **triads**.

Roman numerals (I-ii-iii-IV, etc.) are used to label a chord's location within a key, as well as to indicate the quality (major, minor, diminished) of the chord. Taking a closer look, notice that **major** triads are built on the first (I), fourth (IV), and, fifth (V) notes of the major scale; **minor** triads are built on the second (ii), third (iii), and sixth (vi) notes of the scale; and a **diminished** triad is built on the seventh note (vii°) of the scale. It is important to memorize this sequence of chord types, as it applies to all major scales.

The "cowboy chord" or first position chord versions of C major are as follows:

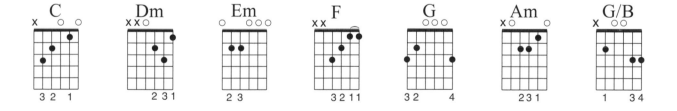

Note that I did not use a diminished chord (B°) for the seventh scale degree, as traditional theory would dictate. For the purposes of this book, the slash chord G/B is more stylistically appropriate. (The seventh degree, B, the bass note of the chord, still serves as a "leading tone"—i.e., a note that resolves to the tonic or root of the scale in a typical chord progression.)

IMPROVISING IN C

The following examples are in the key of C; that is, they use chord progressions derived from a C major scale. Practice playing the chords; then try improvising over them using the C major scale. When beginning to improvise, play the scale ascending and descending, and notice how the notes work over the chords. Then, mix up the notes. It helps to emphasize chord tones.

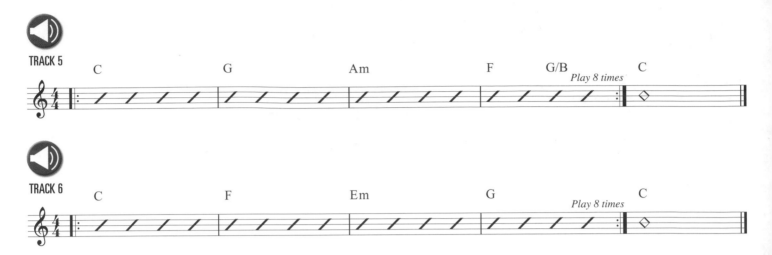

The following licks should give you a feel for how alternate picking along with using the open strings give a country or bluegrass flavor to major scale improvising. These licks are played in **cut time**. Cut time, or "two-beat" as it is called in country music, has two beats per measure, with the half note receiving one beat. On the CD, these go by quite fast. Practice them slowly at first.

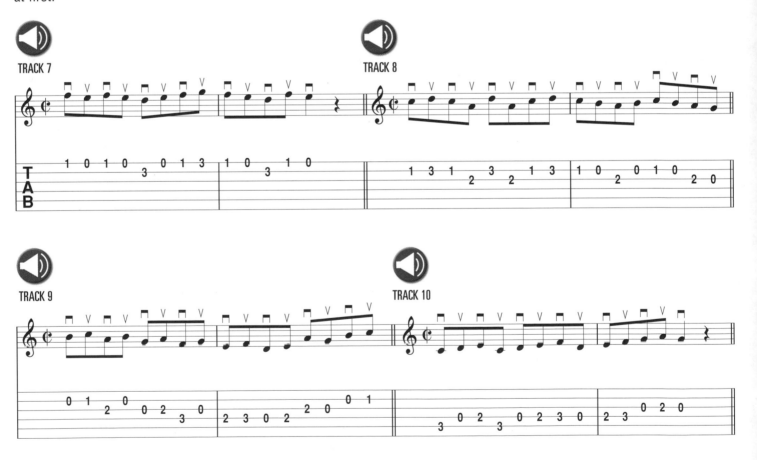

CARTER PICKING

One of the most famous styles of traditional country guitar playing, **Carter picking** was popularized by (and named for) country legend Maybelle Carter of the Carter Family, an influential group of the '20s and '30s. Basically, Carter picking is a solo style of playing: The melody of a song is picked on the lower strings of the guitar, while harmony is added in between these notes, strummed on the higher strings.

This arrangement of Johnny Cash's "I Walk the Line" is a good place to start with Carter picking. The melody should stand out here; it's in the bass. Play it more loudly than the chord strums (on the higher strings) and hold each melody note for its full value—or longer, if need be.

I WALK THE LINE

TRACK 11

Words and Music by John R. Cash

Before we get to "Wildwood Flower," probably the most notable of Maybelle Carter's classics, we need to discuss a couple of new techniques that allow you to "slur" two or more notes together to create a smooth, flowing sound and help give your music flavor and expression. These two **articulations** (ways of playing and connecting notes on the guitar) are the "hammer-on" and the "pull-off."

THE HAMMER-ON

The **hammer-on** is named for the action of the left-hand finger on the fretboard. To play a hammer-on, follow these steps:

- Play the first note as usual. (Fret the note with your left hand; pick the string with your right.)

- Maintain pressure as you quickly use another left-hand finger to press down ("hammer on") onto a higher fret of the same string, sounding the second note.

Hammer-ons can be played from fret to fret, or from an open string to a fretted note. Regardless of fingering, you'll always hammer from a lower to a higher note. Use the initial pick attack (on the first note) to carry the tone.

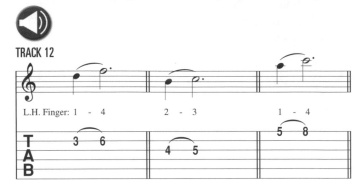

THE PULL-OFF

The **pull-off** is the opposite of the hammer-on. To play a pull-off, follow these steps:

- Play the first note as usual. (Fret the note with your left hand; pick the string with your right.)

- Maintain pressure, as you quickly "pull" that left-hand finger off the string, sounding the second (lower) note on the same string.

Pull-offs can be played from fret to fret, or from a fretted note to an open string. Regardless of fingering, you'll always pull off from a higher to a lower note. Use the initial pick attack (on the first note) to carry the tone.

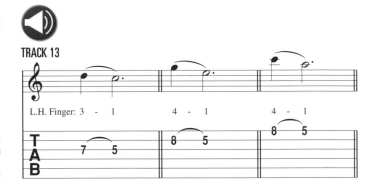

TIP: When possible, place both fingers on their respective frets *before* pulling off from one note to the next.

WHEN PLAYING "WILDWOOD FLOWER"...

This is not a fast song, but practice it slowly to keep a consistent tempo before bringing up the pace a little.

- Keep your left-hand fingers in chord position, except when it's necessary to move them to play certain melody notes.

- Use your third finger to play the A note in the melody when it occurs over the C chord.

- Pick using all downstrokes.

- Have fun with the hammer-ons and pull-offs, which add variety and excitement to the arrangement. Notice that they are all on the D string, between the open string and 2nd fret.

WILDWOOD FLOWER

Words and Music by A.P. Carter
Copyright © 1935 by Peer International Corporation
Copyright Renewed

"BOOM CHICK" RHYTHM

Another popular country technique is sometimes called "boom chick"; this is a style of rhythm guitar frequently associated with Western swing, but it is applicable to a broad range of other styles as well. The "boom chick" rhythm basically calls for hitting the bass note of a chord (the "boom") and then the rest of the chord immediately after (the "chick").

Typically, you alternate between the root and the fifth of the chord for your "boom" notes. This may or may not require a fingering change. On this C chord, for example, the third finger usually moves from C to G, while the rest of the fingers remain on the chord shape.

A great tune for practicing this is "Hey, Good Lookin'" by the great Hank Williams. This song is an excellent example of "boom chick" rhythm. Notice that the D chord in this tune is major instead of minor; this goes against the rules of C major that we have learned so far, but don't be alarmed. This type of substitution is frequently used in popular music. Here, the D chord is part of a II-V turnaround. Although the II-V progression often utilizes a minor ii chord, the major II chord is also commonly used in country music.

When playing this song, use all downstrokes and try muting ever so slightly with the palm of your right hand (see "Palm Muting" on the opposite page). Play rhythm along with the CD; we'll learn the melody next.

TRACK 15

HEY, GOOD LOOKIN'
(RHYTHM)

PALM MUTING

A little muting with the palm of the right hand really add to the "boom chick" effect. **Palm muting** is best achieved by using the side or heel of your picking hand to rest against the bridge, muffling or "muting" the strings as you play.

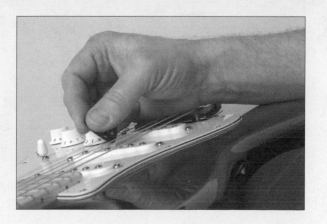

Before we tackle the melody to "Hey, Good Lookin'," let's add another articulation to our repertoire. This time, it's the slide.

THE SLIDE

The **slide** is played by following these steps:

- Pick the first note as usual.

- Maintain pressure, as you move ("slide") your left-hand finger up or down the string to the second note. (The second note is not picked; use the initial pick attack of the first note to carry the tone.)

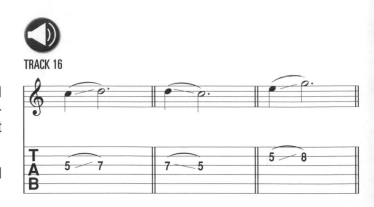

TRACK 16

You can use any finger to slide a note; the first, second, and third fingers are the most common.

THE MAJOR PENTATONIC

Almost the entire melody of "Hey, Good Lookin'" (see opposite page) is based on just fives notes of the C major scale: C, D, E, G, and A. These actually form their own scale, called C major pentatonic.

If we the same numbering system that we used for the major scale, the **major pentatonic** could be defined like this: 1–2–3–5–6. Notice that the 4th and 7th degrees of the major scale are omitted.

The major pentatonic is an extremely effective scale for sounding "country" when improvising. Here's an exercise using the C major pentatonic scale in first position.

TRACK 17

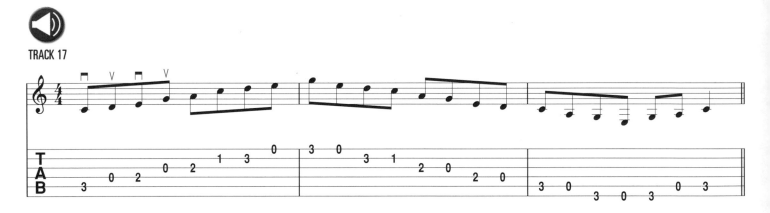

We're going to play the melody to "Hey, Good Lookin'," and then there is going to be a chance for you to "pick awhile" using the C major scale and/or C major pentatonic. Play through these two C pentatonic licks as ideas.

TRACK 18   TRACK 19

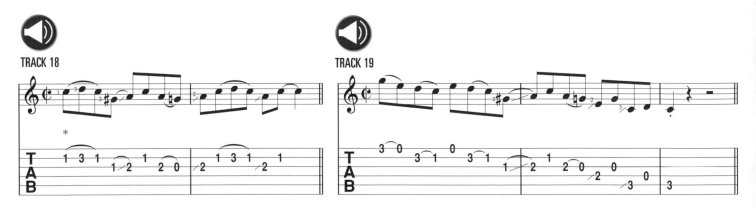

*Hammer-on and pull-off (pick 1st note only).

Notice that the above licks make use of slides "from nowhere"; these are ornamental slides to a main note. To play these, simply begin one or two frets below the indicated fret, pick the string, and slide up to that note quickly.

Play along with the melody of "Hey, Good Lookin'" on the following CD track. The whole song will actually be played twice; the second time through, "pick awhile"—that is, try improvising with the C major scale and/or C major pentatonic. Also, try throwing in the licks you just learned. If you like, just play the melody again, but try adding some variations here and there.

HEY, GOOD LOOKIN'
(MELODY)

TRACK 20

Some other means of articulating notes (as a guitarist in the "country" vein) are the string bend and vibrato.

THE STRING BEND

The **string bend** produces the characteristic "moaning" or vocal-like sound of blues, rock, and country guitar, and makes it possible to change pitch without changing the fret position of the finger. To bend a string, follow these steps:

- Play the first note as usual. (The left-hand 3rd finger is optimal for bending notes.)

- Maintain pressure as you push the string upward or pull it downward to the second, higher note.

- Use your first and second fingers for additional support.

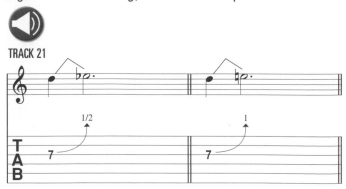

Bends are indicated in music by a pointed slur (and an arrow in tablature). Bending strings works best on electric or steel-string acoustic guitars and is done most easily on the first three strings.

TIP: When bending up to a note, it may help to first establish the correct pitch in your mind. To do this, find the note on the fretboard first and play it; then go back and try bending up to that pitch from the starting note.

VIBRATO

Vibrato can be either a shallow, quick quiver or a wide, earth-shaking move. It's achieved by pushing and pulling the string up and down with your fret hand after sounding a note. This gives the note a more "singing" quality.

Country guitarists apply vibrato as follows:

- Pick the note as usual.

- Maintain pressure as you push and pull the string perpendicular to its length.

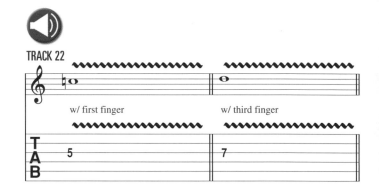

Vibrato is indicated in music by a wavy line above standard notation and tablature.

Now let's play the melody to Alan Jackson's "Chattahoochee." Here are a few tips: 1) The vibrato indicated should be fairly shallow and is added just to give the melody some attitude, 2) the intro riff can be emphasized by picking closer to the bridge to give it the necessary "twang," and 3) in measure 2 of the chorus, let your second finger "roll" from E to A, flattening a bit to play both notes. On the CD, the song is played two times: slow, then fast.

CHATTAHOOCHEE

G MAJOR

Having a good grasp of the major scales in open position allows you not only to play melodies in between your "cowboy chords," but also to improvise in an "idiomatically correct" fashion—in other words, to sound like a country guitarist! A very popular "country" key is the key of G.

To build a G major scale, start with the note G, and apply the major scale pattern (W-W-H-W-W-W-H). To complete this pattern, the F will be sharped.

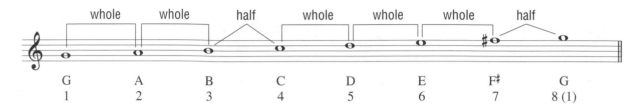

Practice the G major scale in open position. Observe: the **key signature** for G major is one sharp (F#). This means that every F should be played as an F#.

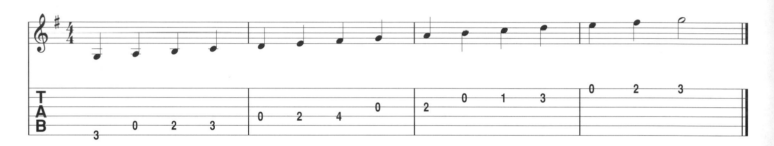

Try these two licks using the G major scale and some of the techniques we've learned so far. Listen to how just a few nuances (like slides or bends) make these scalar licks sound "country":

Here are the "cowboy" chords in the key of G:

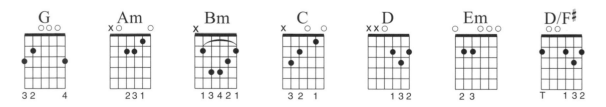

The Bm chord shown here is what's known as a "barre chord." Let's take a moment to discuss these types of chords.

BARRE CHORDS

Barre chords are chords in which two or more strings are depressed using the same finger. Most barre chords cover five or six strings and contain no open strings. The fingering shapes are movable and can be shifted up or down the neck to different positions to produce other chords of the same quality.

A-TYPE BARRE CHORD

One of the most useful movable barre chords is the one based on the open A chord. The root note of this shape is on the fifth string. Therefore, it will be used to play major chords up and down the fifth string.

Follow these steps to form the A-type barre chord:

1. Play an open A chord, using your 3rd finger only: Lay it flat across the second fret, covering strings 2-4.

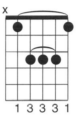

2. Slide this chord shape up on fret, and add your 1st finger across the 1st fret, forming a barre.

Strum all five strings to play your first barre chord. Make sure each string rings out clearly. Strike each note one at a time to test for clarity.

TIP: This fingering can be tricky at first. If you're having trouble elevating the middle knuckle of your 3rd finger, you may want to avoid playing the first string (either by not striking it with the right hand, or by muting it).

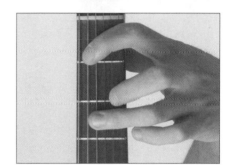

Because its root is at the first fret, this particular barre chord is B♭ major (or A♯ major). You can apply this same shape to any root along the 5th string.

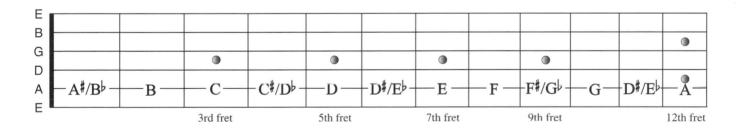

The barre chord shape below is derived from the A-type major barre chord above. You'll notice that it resembles an Am chord. (This is the shape used to play the Bm chord you just learned in the key of G.)

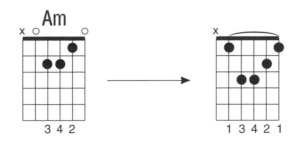

This "A-type" barre chord rendition of the chorus to the country-rock classic "Ramblin' Man" by the Allman Brothers Band is a great exercise for the playing of these chords in the key of G.

RAMBLIN' MAN
(CHORUS)

TRACK 26

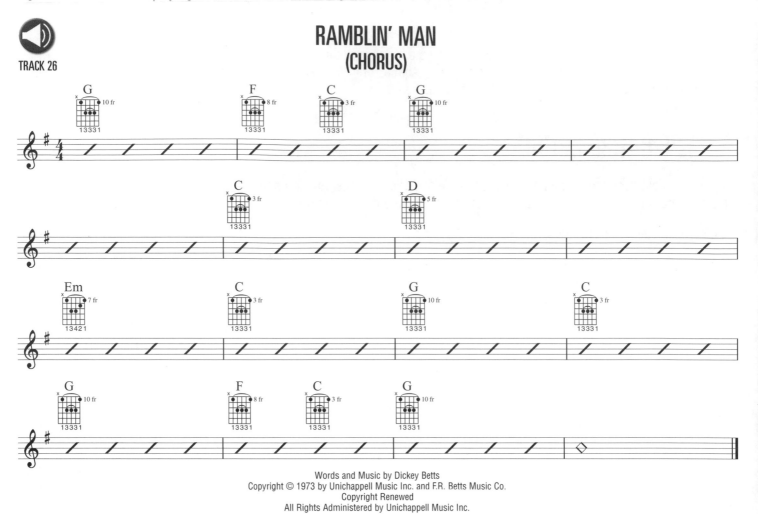

Now let's get back to first position in the key of G. The following exercise utilizes the chords of G major but also introduces the idea of using the hammer-on as a rhythm technique. As in "Wildwood Flower," use all downstrokes and let the chords ring throughout, and you'll have learned a very effective rhythm technique for playing country guitar. After you've played rhythm along with the CD and feel comfortable, switch to playing lead using the G major scale and licks on page 20 as your guide.

HAMMER-ON RHYTHM EXERCISE (IN G)

TRACK 27

*T = Thumb on ⑥

DOUBLE STOPS IN THIRDS

A **double stop** is simply two notes played simultaneously; it's a favorite tool used by country guitarists to harmonize a melody or lick. One of the most common double stops is the interval of the **third**.

Thirds, you may recall, were the building blocks of chords. If we harmonize each note of the G major scale in thirds, we get a series of major and minor thirds consistent with the chords of the major scale.

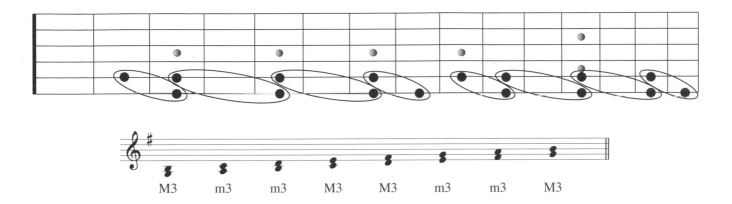

When improvising, it helps to remember this sequence of major and minor thirds. Major and minor thirds feel different from one another on the fretboard, and their shapes change depending on what set of strings they are played.

Play the following double-stop, two-octave exercise, consisting of thirds in G major. When playing the double stops, try these different techniques:

* Using all downstrokes of the pick so that the higher string is struck almost simultaneously with the lower one.
* Using your thumb on the lower string and first finger on the higher string, plucking the strings simultaneously.
* Using your fingers in conjunction with a pick ("hybrid picking"), sounding the lower string with the pick while simultaneously plucking the higher string with the middle finger.

TRACK 28

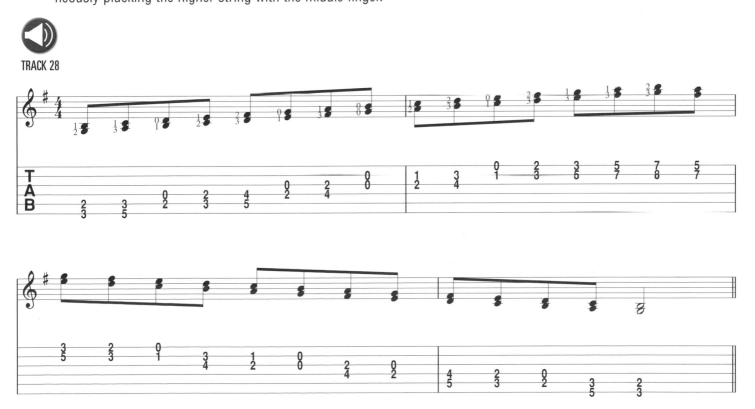

This arrangement of the great Johnny Cash's "Ring of Fire" combines double-stop thirds with some of the other techniques we've learned thus far. While stating the melody in Carter style, feel free to let the chords ring out beyond the bar lines to give the piece a flowing feel.

When playing the passages with double stops, use whatever fingering feels most comfortable. In country, as well as blues and rock, traditional guitar position rules are overruled by the need to utilize articulations that depend on a player's confidence level (slides, vibrato, etc.). So, in other words, the ends justify the means—if your pinky feels wimpy, trudge on with fingerings that are more comfortable.

RING OF FIRE

TRACK 29

This piece also provides an excellent opportunity to experiment with different approaches to picking. Play it through with your thumb and fingers and then with pick and fingers. Notice the mellow sound and softer dynamics of playing with your thumb and fingers versus the more aggressive, brighter sound of the pick with fingers, or "hybrid picking," approach.

G MAJOR PENTATONIC
WITH ADDED ♭3RD

As we learned in the key of C, the major pentatonic is an excellent tool for sounding "country." The G major pentatonic scale in first position is particularly important because it forms a "box," visually speaking, that is easily moved up the neck to form the major pentatonic scale in other keys as well (we'll see more of this later). Adding a flat 3rd (B♭) to our G major pentatonic scale provides an extra "flavor" useful for melodies and improvisation.

Let's take a look at what this "box" looks like. Note the triangles around the added ♭3rd.

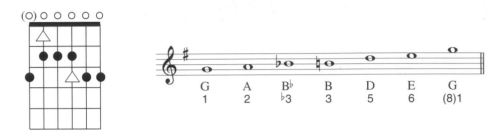

Now, let's hear what it sounds like.

TRACK 30

Try these two licks using the G major pentatonic scale with the added ♭3rd and some of the articulation techniques we've come across. In the first lick, you may find the whole-step bend to be a challenge if you're not playing electric. Try substituting a slide for the bend, if you prefer.

TRACK 31
FAST/SLOW

TRACK 32
FAST/SLOW

Our next tune, "Sugarfoot Rag," is in the fiddle-tune tradition of fast, flat-pickin' classics that are a lot of fun to play. One of the great things about fiddle tunes is that, at a slow tempo, they're relatively easy; then, as your technique develops, you can speed them up until you can't see your hands move!

The tune was written and performed by country guitar pioneer Hank Garland and more recently popularized by the great Junior Brown. This arrangement in G is going to require a little bit of dexterity, but if you start slowly, you should have no problem.

The CD includes both a moderate, melody-only version of "Sugarfoot Rag," and a faster, full-band version. Play along first at a moderate tempo; use alternate picking, and make sure that the double-stop slides are flowing and musical. Then speed it up a bit. A jam track version (without the melody) follows—"pick awhile" using the G major pentatonic scale, the above licks, and all the skills we've learned so far.

SUGARFOOT RAG

TRACK 33
SLOW/FAST

TRACK 34

D MAJOR

In keeping with our theme of learning our first position scales, let's move on to the key of D. To build a D major scale, start with the note D and apply the major scale pattern (W-W-H-W-W-W-H):

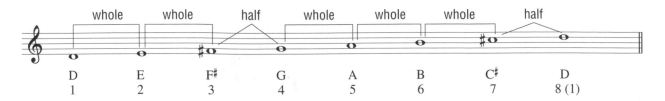

	whole	whole	half	whole	whole	whole	half
D	E	F#	G	A	B	C#	D
1	2	3	4	5	6	7	8 (1)

Practice the D major scale ascending and descending in first position. Observe: the key signature is two sharps (F# and C#).

If you place your first finger at the second fret, you'll be playing in what is called **second position**. The principal advantage of playing in second position lies in the ease with which certain passages can be fingered.

Try playing a D major scale again, this time in second position.

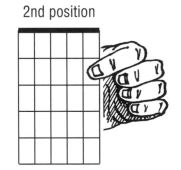

2nd position

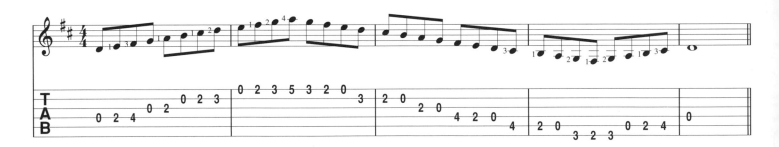

Notice that the open strings can still be played in second position. Many times, a scale or lick in "open position" is more easily fingered by moving your hand up to the second fret—i.e., playing in second position.

Before we move on, let's talk about another element that will help us with our country sound. The organization and delivery of notes in a solo is called "phrasing," and the use of triplets is an essential phrasing tool in most popular music, including country.

Triplets subdivide a unit (like a quarter note) into three parts instead of two parts. In 4/4 or 3/4 time, two eighth notes get one count, so an eighth-note triplet will also get one count:

Triplets are beamed together with a number "3". To count a triplet, simply say the word "tri-pl-et" during one beat. Tap your foot to the beat, and count aloud:

Count: 1   2   tri - pl - et   4   tri - pl - et   tri - pl - et   3   4   1   2   &   tri - pl - et   4

LICKS

Here are some bluegrass-tinged licks using triplets. The open string pull-offs and half-note bends in this key are widely used in country and have a sound all of their own. Everyone from Chet Atkins to Vince Gill has taken advantage of this unique sound. These licks are played in second position.

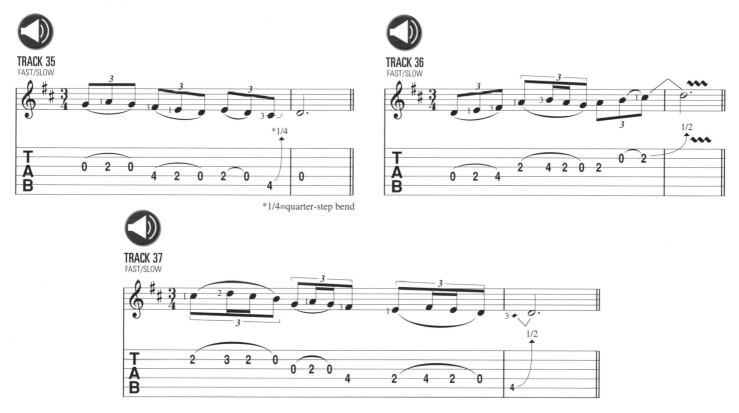

TRACK 35
FAST/SLOW

*1/4=quarter-step bend

TRACK 36
FAST/SLOW

TRACK 37
FAST/SLOW

CHORDS

Here are the "cowboy" chords you should know in D major:

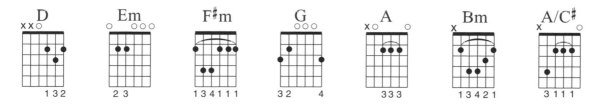

D	Em	F#m	G	A	Bm	A/C#
1 3 2	2 3	1 3 4 1 1 1	3 2 4	3 3 3	1 3 4 2 1	3 1 1 1

The F#m chord pictured here is based on an E-type barre chord. Let's take a moment to discuss these types of chords.

E-TYPE BARRE CHORD

The open E chord can also be converted into a barre chord. This shape will have its root on the sixth string. Follow these steps:

1. Play an open E chord, but use your 2nd, 3rd, and 4th fingers.

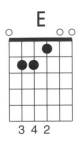

E
3 4 2

2. Slide this chord shape up one fret, and add your 1st finger across the 1st fret, forming a barre.

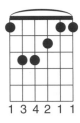

1 3 4 2 1 1

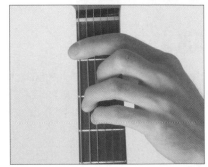

Strum all six strings, and make sure each string rings out clearly. Strike each note one at a time to test for clarity.

This particular barre chord is F major because its root is F on the sixth string. You can apply this same shape to any root note along the sixth string. Practice this shape up and down the neck:

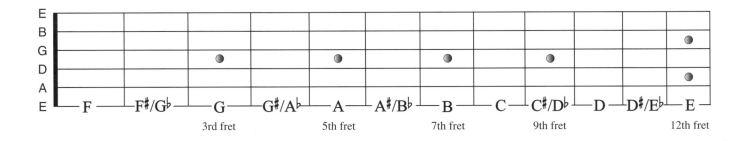

If you subtract your second finger from the "E-type" major barre chord, you have the "E-type" minor barre chord:

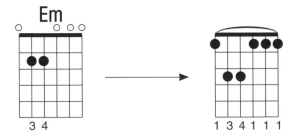

Em
3 4

1 3 4 1 1 1

TIP: An alternative fingering that many guitarists use for E-type barre chords, particularly on the lower frets, is to form a partial barre with the 1st finger across the top strings, letting the thumb wrap around the top of the neck to play the bottom string. This common "shortcut" can be easier on the left hand than a full barre, and is perfectly acceptable in country, folk, rock and other popular guitar styles.

T 3 4 2 1 1

T 3 4 1 1 1

Strum along with this example of "Mercury Blues," using all "E-type" barre chords:

MERCURY BLUES

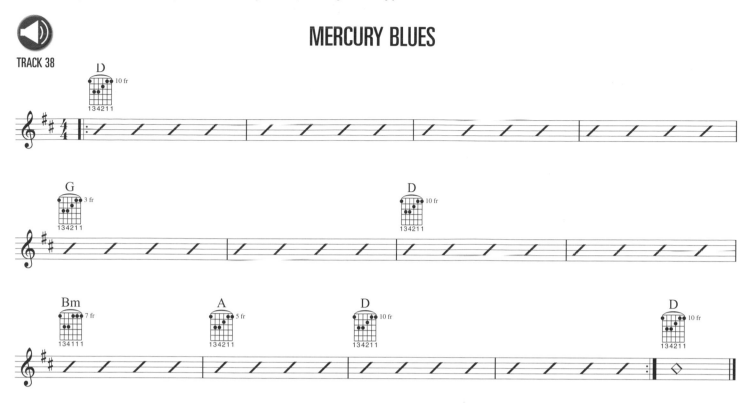

The following exercise uses a famous chord progression (I–vi–IV–V) that is very common in all popular music, including country. This exercise also provides an excellent opportunity to practice using both the E-type and A-type barre chord voicings. Try picking each string individually and letting the notes ring to achieve an arpeggio-type effect.

I–vi–IV–V

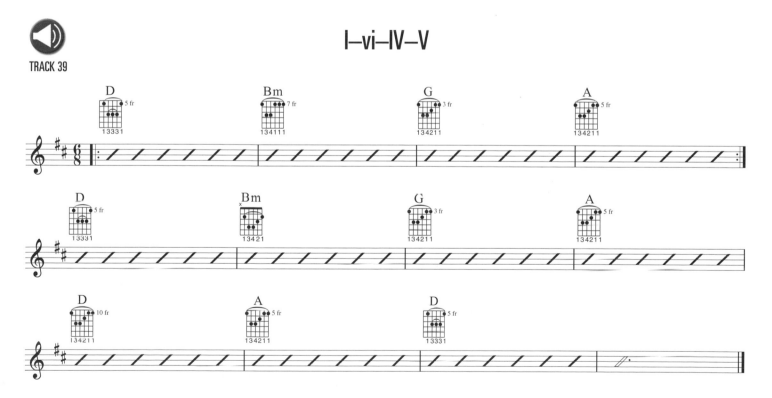

SUS CHORDS & SEVENTH CHORDS

Getting back to our "cowboy" chords in D major, let's add two more flavors to further your country rhythm repertoire: sus chords and seventh chords.

In **sus chords**, you replace the third of the a chord with the fourth, as in sus4 (pronounced "suss four"), or sometimes with the second, as in sus2. The resulting sound is incomplete or unresolved but creates an interesting quality that is neither major nor minor.

Dsus4   Dsus2

Here are some examples:

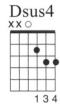  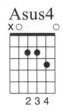 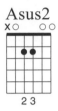 

Dsus4   Dsus2   Asus4   Asus2   Gsus4

Seventh chords are comprised of four notes: the three notes of a triad plus a major or minor seventh interval.

The most commonly used seventh chords in country music contain the added minor seventh. For example, if we take our D major triad (D-F#-A), and add a minor seventh interval (C♮), we get D7. This is also referred to as a **dominant seventh** chord:

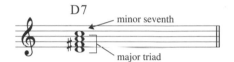

D7
minor seventh
major triad

Here are some "cowboy" chord voicings of dominant seventh chords:

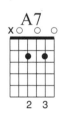  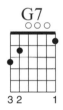 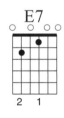 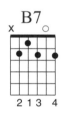

D7   A7   G7   E7   B7

The "A-type" and "E-type" barre chord versions of the dominant seventh look like this:

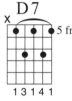 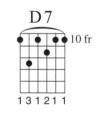

D7 5 fr   D7 10 fr

If we start with a minor triad and a minor seventh interval, we get what is called a **minor seventh** chord. For example, if we take an E minor triad (E-G-B) and add a minor seventh interval (D), we get Em7.

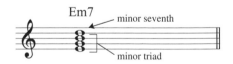

Em7
minor seventh
minor triad

Some "cowboy" chord examples of minor seventh chords:

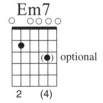 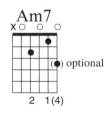  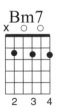

Em7   Am7   Dm7   Bm7

The "A-type" and "E-type" barre chord versions of the minor seventh chord look like this:

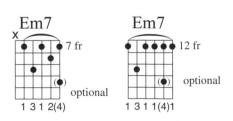

Em7 7 fr   Em7 12 fr

Play the following waltz in D, strumming along with the combination of major, minor, sus, dominant seventh, and minor seventh chords. After playing the chords twice through the arrangement, take two choruses to "pick awhile" using the D major scale and the licks in D as your guide.

TRACK 40

DSUS WALTZ

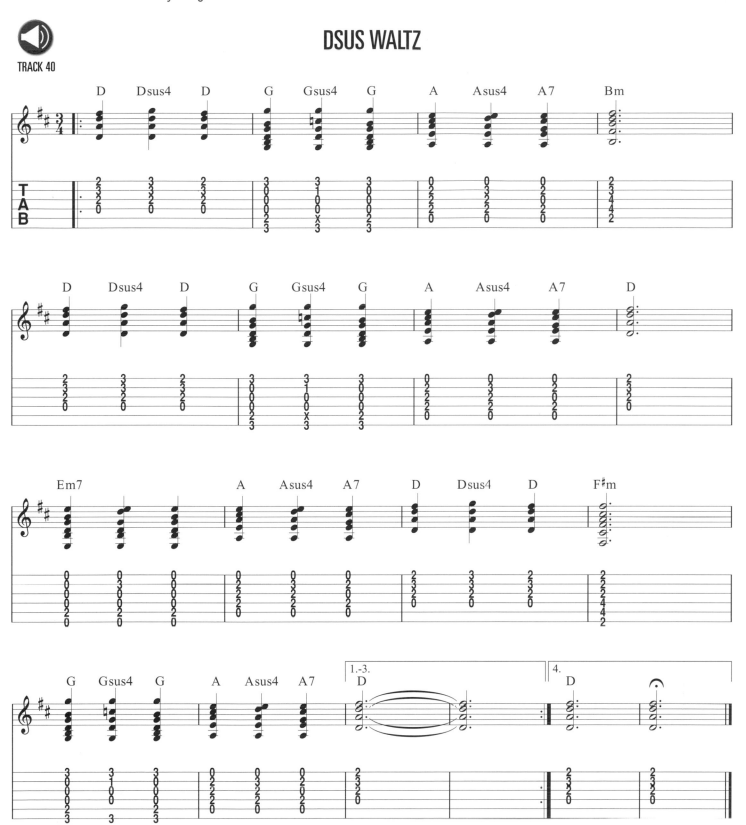

Buck Owens and his right-hand man, guitarist and fiddler Don Rich, were a mighty influential force in country music. This arrangement of their 1965 chart-topper "Buckaroo" gives us a good example of working in the suspended 4th notes for effect.

This tune presents some interesting challenges from a technical standpoint. The main melody is stated in D in first position and then the same chordal shape that encompasses all the melody notes moves up to the fifth fret to G. This is done by barring your first finger and making the "open D"-shape with your third, fourth, and second fingers. To get the sus4 when in the G position, barre across with your fourth finger to catch the note (C).

Make all the notes ring well beyond their bar line to get a nice flowing feel. You may want to experiment with some of the picking variations, particularly the hybrid (pick & fingers) technique discussed earlier.

Notice that the song ends with a D6/9 chord, a familiar ending chord in many country and rockabilly songs. The 6/9 ("six-nine") is what is called an **extended chord**; i.e., a chord that includes notes beyond the seventh scale degree. We'll see more of these chords later. For now, just realize that the notes comprising this D6/9 chord are: root (D), 3rd (F♯), 6th (B), 9th (E), 5th (A), and root (D).

BUCKAROO

TRACK 41

Words and Music by Bob Morris
Copyright © 1965 Sony/ATV Songs LLC
Copyright Renewed
All Rights Administered by Sony/ATV Music Publishing, 8 Music Square West, Nashville, TN 37203

GRACE NOTES

Grace notes are an excellent way to add some personality to melodies or improvisations in any style. Grace notes are basically a quick note played right before an intended note. In fact, they happen so fast that they are indicated with a small note (♪) before the intended note. We've used grace notes, to some extent, with our bends thus far, but here are some other grace note examples:

TRACK 42

This arrangement of "Forever and Ever, Amen," made famous by Randy Travis, has plenty of grace notes. The double-stop grace notes are of particular interest as they are very "country" sounding. You may employ any picking style that you feel comfortable with, but the hybrid (pick-and-fingers) technique is highly encouraged as it will prepare you for further techniques unique to country guitar stylings. This song is played in second position throughout.

FOREVER AND EVER, AMEN

TRACK 43

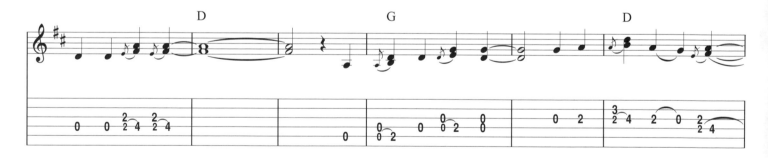

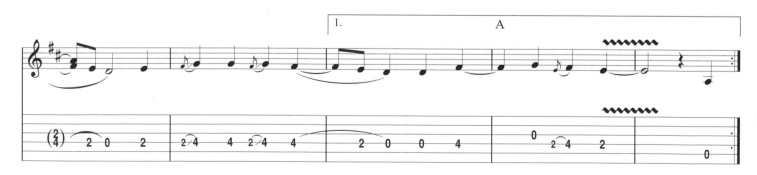

Words and Music by Paul Overstreet and Don Schlitz

D MAJOR PENTATONIC
WITH ADDED ♭3RD

Let's add another scale to our improvisational repertoire: D major pentatonic scale with an added flat 3rd. This "country"-sounding scale can come in quite handy, as we'll soon see.

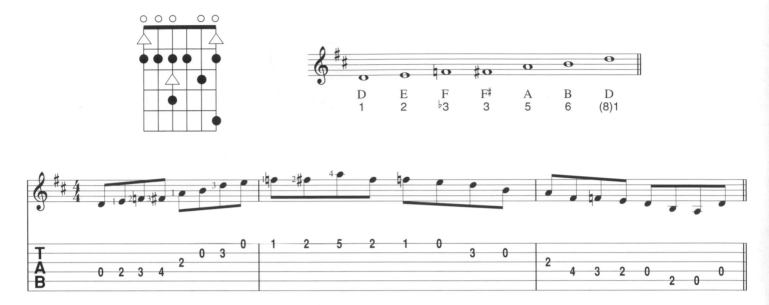

These licks should get you started with some possibilities. Feel free to find your own fingerings for these, using first or second position, or both.

TRACK 44
FAST/SLOW

TRACK 45
FAST/SLOW

TRACK 46

Here's a jam track version of "Forever and Ever, Amen." Take a few passes to "pick awhile" over it. Try these two approaches:

1. Use the D major scale and the licks you've learned. Be careful on the E7 chord, though, as it takes you out of the usual D major tonality. Try staying away from the G note or add a G♯ for just that measure, and you should be fine.

2. Another way of dealing with the E7 chord is to use only the notes of the D major pentatonic with added flat 3rd. Many players in country and in other genres are able to get through tricky chord changes by using just this scale.

A MAJOR

Let's proceed with our study of major scales with another popular key for country music, the key of A.

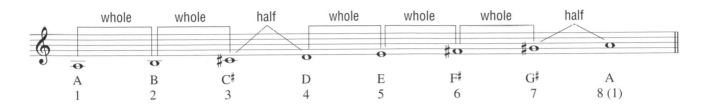

Practice the two-octave A major scale ascending and descending. Remember: the key signature for A major is three sharps (F#, C#, G#). The fingering shown mixes first and second position.

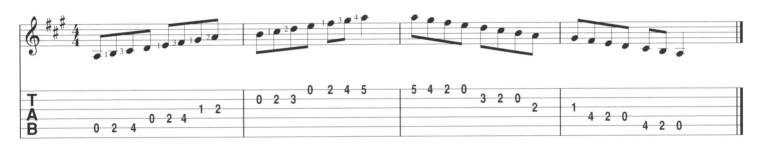

Here some licks in A that mimic the sound of a popular instrument in country music, the **pedal steel** guitar. Pedal steel is an instrument that utilizes pedals to bend the pitches of the strings with your feet, while a steel bar is used as a slide on the strings. Many country guitarists have learned to imitate the sound of a pedal steel guitar very effectively. We will continue to explore these kinds of licks in this book, but here are a few to get you started:

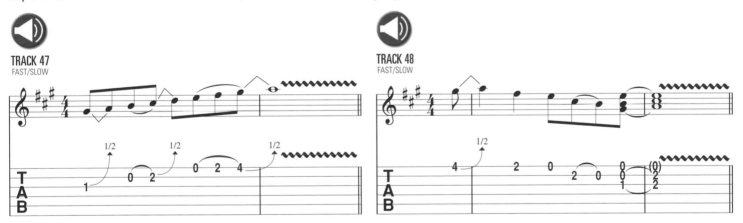

Here are "cowboy" chord voicings of A major:

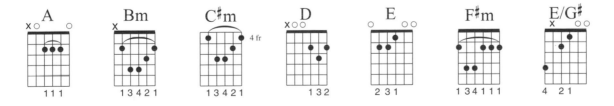

Let's practice our "cowboy" chords and other A major chords using a fingerstyle technique named after one of the greats of country guitar, Merle Travis.

TRAVIS PICKING

Travis picking is a fingerstyle technique. The basic approach has two main characteristics:

- The thumb alternates between two bass strings, either on beats 1 and 3 or in steady quarter notes.

- The fingers pluck the higher strings, usually between the bass notes (on the upbeats).

The result is a driving rhythmic feel that was the backbone of the style of not only Merle Travis, but Chet Atkins and many others. Although Merle and Chet used thumbpicks, this technique can also be effectively played using hybrid picking—but let's start out with just our fingers to get the hang of it. The right-hand finger and thumb letters used in this book are based on the internationally accepted system of Spanish words and letters.

p	pulgar	=	thumb
i	indice	=	index finger
m	media	=	middle finger
a	anular	=	ring finger

Practice each of the two main Travis picking patterns below. Notice the difference in the use of the thumb bass notes.

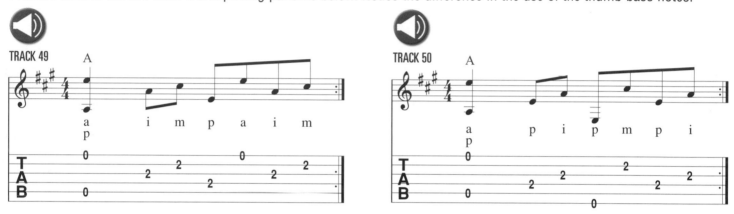

This exercise uses a few different versions of Travis picking in the key of A. Try it slowly by yourself at first, and then when you are more comfortable, play along with the CD. If you add some palm muting (with your picking hand) on the bass notes, letting all the other notes ring, you'll achieve the sound that Merle and Chet made famous!

PICKIN' IN A

Now go back and use the A major scale and the pedal steel licks to a "pick awhile" over the chord changes to the above Travis picking exercise.

In addition to being a great accompaniment pattern to a vocal or other instrument, you may also use a variation on Travis picking to play melodies while keeping the driving bass line going, à la Merle and Chet.

Notice that the following arrangement of the classic "Freight Train" is written *in divisi*—i.e., as two parts. The thumb (p) will play the lower part, and your index (i) and middle (m) fingers will play the melody and additional harmony notes that make up the higher part. You may also hybrid pick this arrangement by substituting the thumb with the pick and the index and middle fingers with your middle and ring fingers, respectively.

Once you start to feel comfortable with this piece, try palm muting the lower part while letting the higher part "ring out."

FREIGHT TRAIN

TRACK 52
FAST/SLOW

MOVABLE SCALES

You already know how to play many scales in open position. To become a skillful soloist in country or in any other genre, you must learn to play scales anywhere on the fingerboard.

The concept of **movable scales** is similar to the concept of barre chords. For each scale (e.g., major, major pentatonic with ♭3rd, etc.), you will learn two movable patterns, one with its tonic on the sixth string and another with its tonic on the fifth string. By using these tonics as a point of reference, you can move the scales up and down the neck to accommodate any key. Simply match one of the tonics to its respective note on the fingerboard, and the rest of the pattern follows accordingly.

MAJOR

Let us take a look at movable major scales, starting with the key of A. Tonics are indicated with an open circle.

Tonic on 6th string

Country guitar pioneer Jimmy Bryant would often add some chromatic notes (a half step above or below scale tones) when playing the major scale, to add some of his customary "fire" to melodies or leads, as in this segment which is reminiscent of one of his legendary instrumental pieces recorded with Speedy West.

Jimmy Bryant-Style Lick #1

TRACK 53
FAST/SLOW

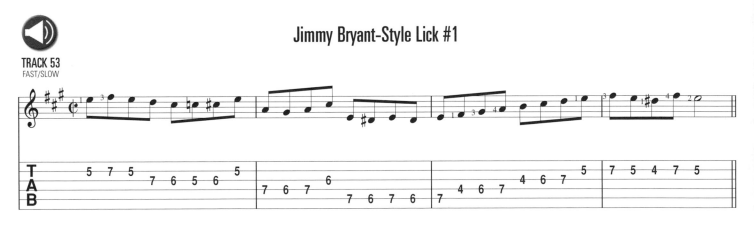

Tonic on 5th string

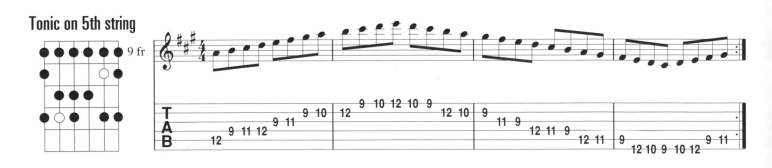

42

Here is another Jimmy Bryant -style major lick, this time in the 9th position.

Jimmy Bryant-Style Lick #2

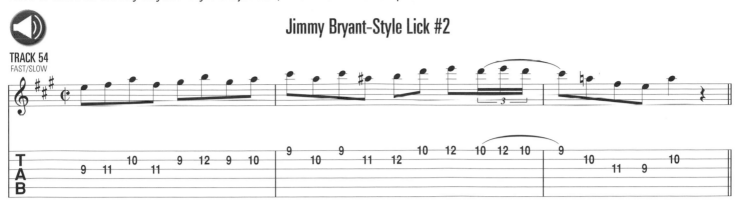

MAJOR PENTATONIC WITH ADDED ♭3RD

As mentioned earlier, the G major pentatonic scale with added flat third forms a "box" shape that is easily moved up the neck. Here is that shape again, this time in the 2nd position, forming the A major pentatonic scale with added flat third (root on the 6th string). Note the triangles, which indicate the flatted third, and the encircled notes, which form a major triad (A major in second position). The latter is a handy visual aid for using this scale when soloing.

Tonic on 6th string

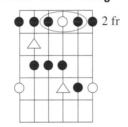

This scale, in this position, is particularly "pedal-steel" friendly, meaning it's great for those style licks. Here are some examples:

- The first lick requires you to bend the G string up a whole step and keep it there for most of the measure. This presents a bit of a challenge at first, but playing along with the CD should help you get it right.

- The second lick has you playing a pre-bent note and then bringing it back down to pitch, for a "pedal steel" type effect, very much in the vein of country/rock guitar pioneer James Burton.

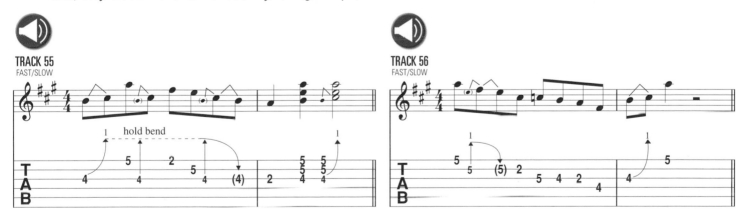

This pattern has its root on the 5th string. In A, that takes us up to the 9th fret. Note the A major triad (encircled) that resembles an "open D" chord shape. This is another handy visual aid for finding this scale for soloing.

Tonic on 5th string

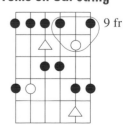

43

CHICKEN PICKIN'

The following licks, based on the A major pentatonic (with ♭3rd) pattern on the 5th string, incorporate a technique called **chicken pickin'**. Chicken pickin' is a technique that involves muting notes, or choking them, to produce a percussive snap that, to many listeners, conjures up the sound of a chicken "clucking."

There are a number of ways to create the chicken pickin' sound:

- Use the side of your thumb on your picking hand to mute or "choke" a note as you pick down (⊓), and let the same note ring as you pick it with an upstroke (V). Repeat this process rapidly.

TRACK 57
FAST/SLOW

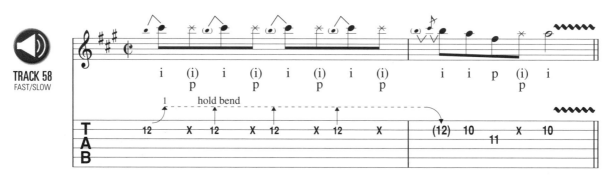

- Use your thumb and first finger à la country-flavored rock guitar great Mark Knopfler. This is achieved by picking a note with our first finger (i) then plucking the same note again with your thumb (p) but with your first finger right behind it, actually on the same string, muting it.

TRACK 58
FAST/SLOW

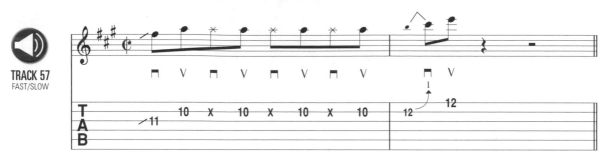

- Use a hybrid picking technique; basically, do the same thing as above, but replace your thumb (p) with the flat pick and your first finger (i) with your middle finger (m). Note that having a little bit of nail on your middle finger allows you to snap the string a little more effectively. Let's hear the same lick above using this technique, and notice how bright and aggressive it sounds in comparison to the thumb-and-fingers approach.

TRACK 59
FAST/SLOW

"Country Gentleman" is a tune written and performed by the country gentleman himself, Chet Atkins. The legendary, English-born country guitarist Albert Lee also recorded this tune, and this arrangement draws from his rendition, which features a lot techniques we've learned thus far. We also have three new chords in this arrangement:

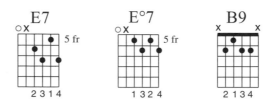

Notice the B9, which is another extended chord. It's actually a **dominant ninth** chord; that is, a dominant seventh chord with another major third stacked on top of the seventh scale degree.

"Country Gentleman" requires either fingerpicking or hybrid picking in sections indicating two parts. The single-note lines can be flatpicked or played with fingers. Notice the sections with the chicken pickin'; feel free to experiment with the different chicken pickin' techniques we discussed. (The CD features a hybrid picking performance of this tune.)

COUNTRY GENTLEMAN

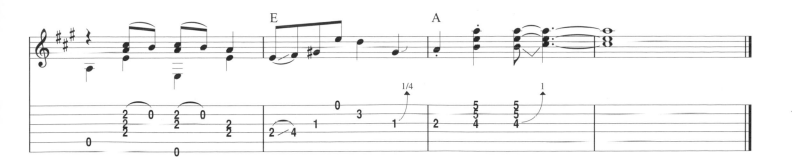

Now, using the movable scales and/or scales in open position, along with the licks we've learned thus far, "pick awhile" over the rhythm track for "Country Gentleman." As a guide to which scales to use over the chords, here are some suggestions:

A major pentatonic with added flat 3rd	over all chords
A major	over A and E chords
D major	over D chords
D major pentatonic with added flat 3rd	over D7
B major pentatonic with added flat 3rd	over B9 or B7
E major pentatonic with added flat 3rd	over E chords

TRACK 61

COUNTRY GENTLEMAN (RHYTHM)

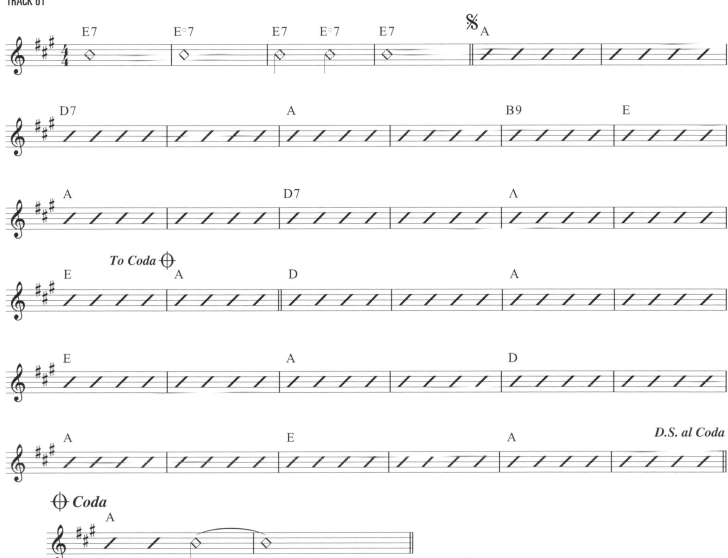

TWELVE-BAR BLUES

The **twelve-bar blues** is a song form used often in country music, from western swing to bluegrass and all points in between.

A basic blues is a 12-measure form containing three chords: the I, IV, and V chords of the chosen key. In the key of A major, this would be A (I), D (IV), and E(V). More often than not, these chords would be dominant sevenths. Here's a basic blues in A:

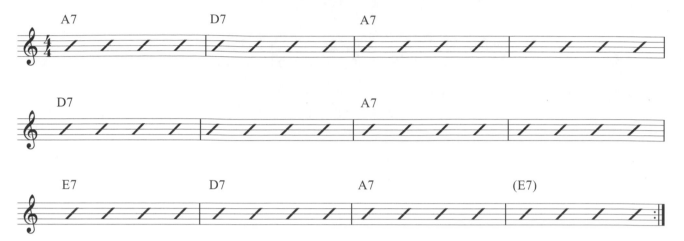

This twelve-bar form would constitute a verse or chorus of a blues, and could be repeated ad infinitum to create a complete song.

THE SHUFFLE RHYTHM

The shuffle rhythm is often used when playing blues in country music. In this rhythm, eighth notes are played unevenly; the first note is twice as long as the second:

The following rhythm patterns are widely used by country guitarists when playing a shuffle or rockabilly-flavored piece. When playing these, try several different approaches with your strumming hand: 1) all downstrokes, 2) accenting the upbeats with upstrokes.

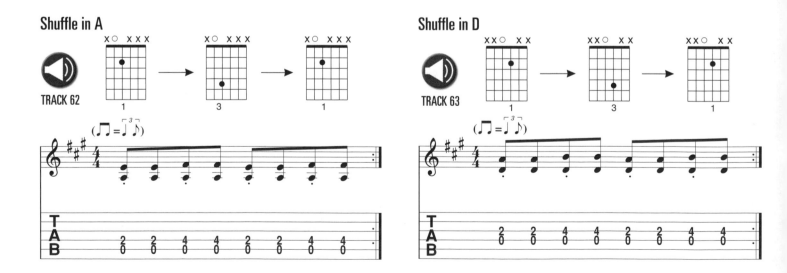

Shuffle in E

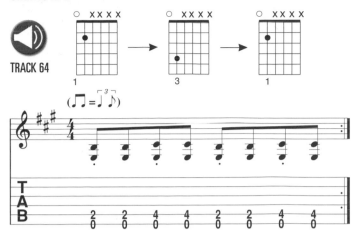

Using the shuffle rhythm patterns you just learned—actually, a slight variation—play along with this arrangement of Hank Williams Sr.'s "Move It On Over."

MOVE IT ON OVER

THE BLUES SCALE

To solo over a blues, you will find the major pentatonic scale with the added flat 3rd works very well. Another great scale for playing over a blues is the blues scale itself. The **blues scale** is identical to the major pentatonic scale with the added flat third, but the location of the tonic is different. In fact, another name for the blues scale is a minor pentatonic scale (1-♭3-4-5-7) with an added flat 5th. In A, the minor pentatonic would be A, C, D, E, G, and the added flat fifth would be E♭.

Here is the blues scale in A, with the tonic on the 6th string. Notice the flatted 5th is indicated by the triangle.

Tonic on 6th string

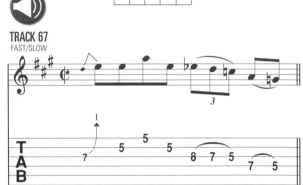

Here are some licks using this scale in the fifth position.

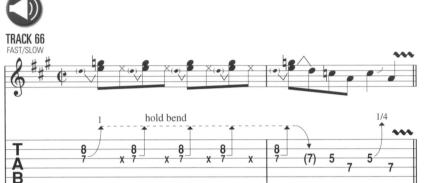

Tonic on 5th string

Here is the blues scale with its tonic on the 5th string. In A, you can play it at the 12th fret, or in open position.

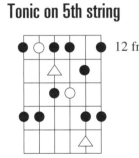

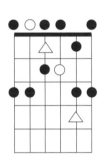

Here are some licks using both positions of the blues scale with its tonic on the fifth string.

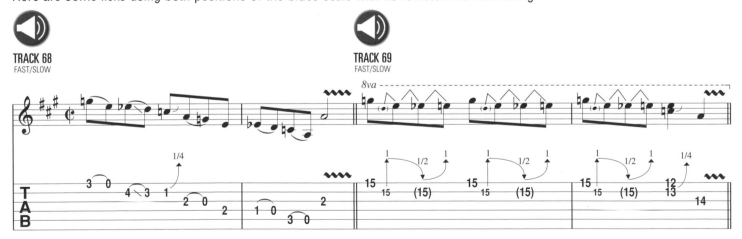

Go back to "Move It On Over" (page 49), and try some of these licks as well as making up some of your own with the blues scale as you "pick awhile" over this jam track.

TRACK 70

The blues scale is also a very effective tool for soloing over a tune in a minor key. Although it seems the vast majority of the most popular country tunes are in major keys, "Sixteen Tons" is an example of a classic country tune in a minor key. Originally penned by Merle Travis himself, the following arrangement includes some Travis picking and provides an opportunity for you to use the blues scale or—by omitting the flat 5th—the minor pentatonic to "pick awhile" over the chord changes. Play with the chordal arrangement twice, and then take two times through the arrangement to solo with the A blues scale or A minor pentatonic, using some of the licks you've learned so far as a guide.

- Notice that the thumb is used on your left hand in this arrangement to hit the F note on the E string at the first fret.

- As with earlier Travis selections in this book, "Sixteen Tons" is written *in divisi*—i.e., as two parts. In this arrangement, the lower part (played with the thumb, or with the pick if hybrid picking) occasionally hits more than just one bass note. This is done to create a fuller sound; aim to strike both strings at the same time with your thumb or with the pick.

- The ending Am6/9 chord is a classic "minor tune" conclusion.

SIXTEEN TONS

TRACK 71

Words and Music by Merle Travis
Copyright © 1947 by Unichappell Music Inc. and Elvis Presley Music
Copyright Renewed
All Rights Administered by Unichappell Music Inc.

MOVABLE SHUFFLE PATTERNS

We can move our shuffle rhythm patterns in the same way we move our barre chords and scales. These two patterns are based on the sixth string and fifth string, respectively.

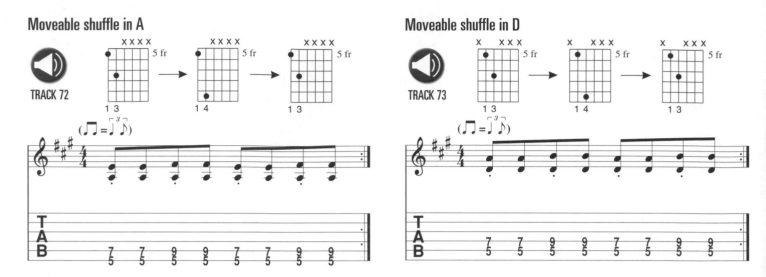

Moveable shuffle in A

TRACK 72

Moveable shuffle in D

TRACK 73

You can also play these rhythm patterns without the shuffle rhythm to achieve a more rockabilly feel. The following arrangement of "The Race Is On," a classic tune made famous by everyone from George Jones to English roots-rocker Dave Edmunds, uses the movable chord forms above in more of a rockabilly fashion.

To add a percussive, locomotive-type feel, release the pressure of your left hand as you finger the chords on the "and"—i.e., on the upstrokes (∨). This "staccato" touch adds the right attitude to this style of rhythm playing.

TRACK 74

THE RACE IS ON

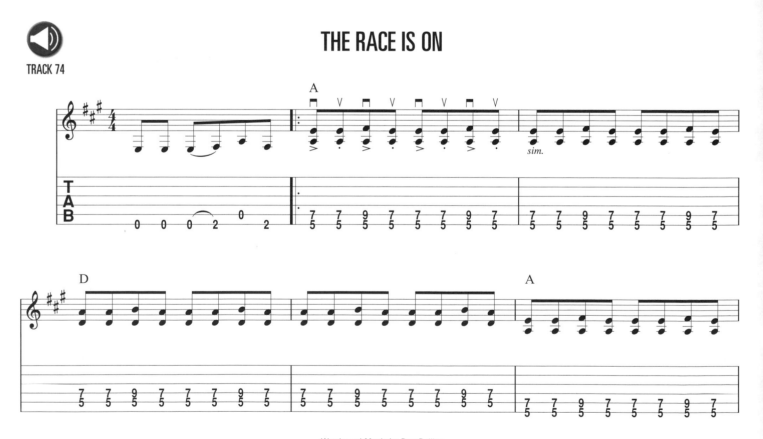

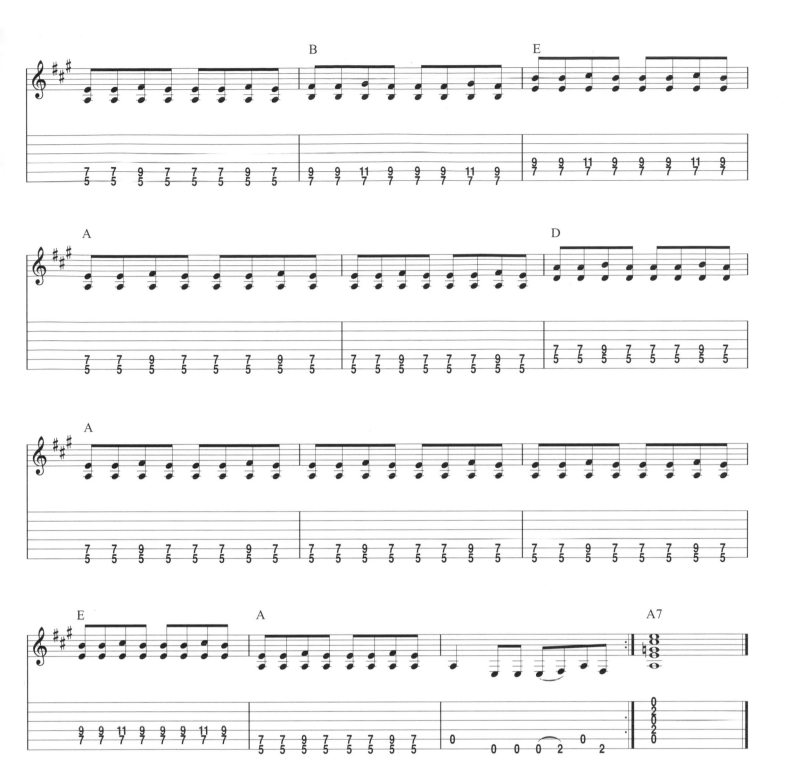

EXTENDING AND BLENDING SCALES

Notes of a scale can be found all over the neck, and if you were to see them all at once, it might be a confusing and intimidating experience! So it is sometimes easier to identify scales by their location within a corresponding chord shape or other visually identifiable position (like the "box" position of the major and minor pentatonic scales). You can extend the position of a scale in a number of ways, but to avoid the "intimidation" factor of seeing a myriad of note options, let's concentrate on one very common extension of our "box" position of the major and minor pentatonic scales (to which we've added the flat 3rd and flat 5th, respectively).

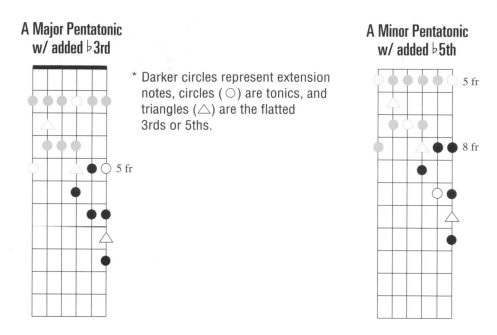

A Major Pentatonic w/ added ♭3rd

A Minor Pentatonic w/ added ♭5th

* Darker circles represent extension notes, circles (○) are tonics, and triangles (△) are the flatted 3rds or 5ths.

Here are some licks using the major and minor pentatonic scale extensions above.

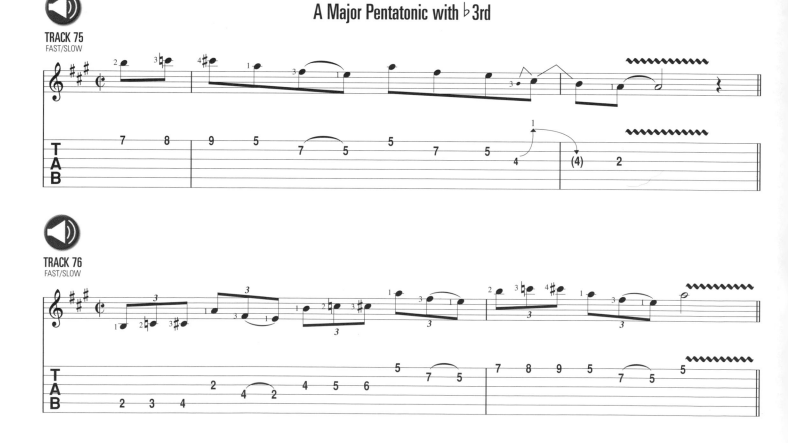

A Major Pentatonic with ♭3rd

TRACK 75
FAST/SLOW

TRACK 76
FAST/SLOW

A Minor Pentatonic with ♭5th (Blues Scale)

A great way to allow you to solo effectively in modern country, which is comprised of everything from Western swing to full-on rock 'n' roll, is to combine the notes from the major pentatonic scale (with added flat 3rd) and the minor pentatonic scale (with added flat 5th; i.e., the blues scale). Having all of these notes at your command—in addition to getting as many "open" strings involved in your licks or riffs as possible—will bring you a long way towards being a convincing country guitar soloist.

The following licks combine both scales and utilize some open strings in the style of country guitar icon Albert Lee.

Albert Lee-Style Licks

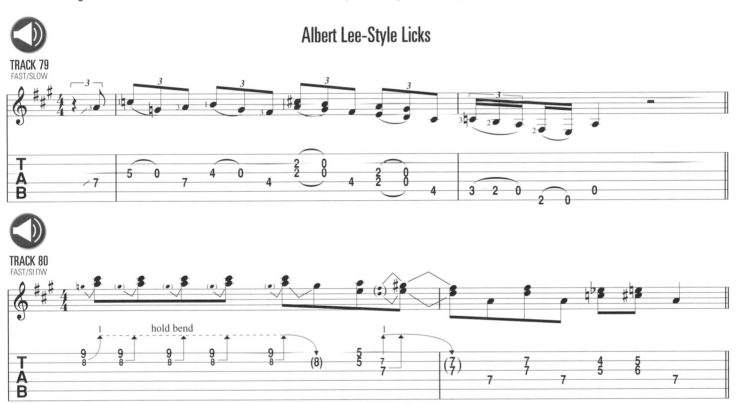

Now let's practice our newfound soloing ideas on "The Race Is On" (pp. 52-53). Here are some ideas on what scales to use to solo over the chords:

A major pentatonic (with added ♭3rd) A blues	over all chords
D major pentatonic (with added ♭3rd) D blues	over D chords
B major pentatonic (with added ♭3rd) B blues	over B chord
E major pentatonic (with added ♭3rd) E blues	over E chords

 "Pick awhile" using some of the licks that correspond with the scales above on "The Race Is On." Start with the A-based ideas (since they'll work over the entire tune), then add the others as you get more comfortable.

TRACK 81

RIFFS AND LICKS IN E

Because the blues scale with its tonic on the sixth string is a common place to find country licks and riffs in any key, the fact that when you play in the key of E you are in open, or first position, makes it even more country friendly because of the open strings involved.

The following are some famous licks and riffs from some country greats:

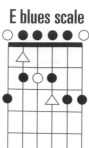

E blues scale

JAMES BURTON'S "SUSIE-Q" RIFF

TRACK 82

*P.M. throughout

*downstemmed notes only

Words and Music by Dale Hawkins, Stan Lewis and Eleanor Broadwater
Copyright © 1957 (Renewed) by Arc Music Corporation (BMI)

MYSTERY TRAIN

TRACK 83

*P.M. throughout

*downstemmed notes only

Words and Music by Sam C. Phillips and Herman Parker Jr.
Copyright © 1955 by Unichappell Music Inc.
Copyright Renewed

LITTLE SISTER

TRACK 84

Words and Music by Doc Pomus and Mort Shuman
Copyright © 1961 by Elvis Presley Music, Inc.
Copyright Renewed and Assigned to Elvis Presley Music
All Rights Administered by Cherry River Music Co. and Chrysalis Songs

FOLSOM PRISON BLUES (INTRO)

BOOGIE PATTERNS

A single-note, repetitive riff called a **boogie pattern** is common in country music. Here is an example of a boogie pattern in E.

TRACK 86

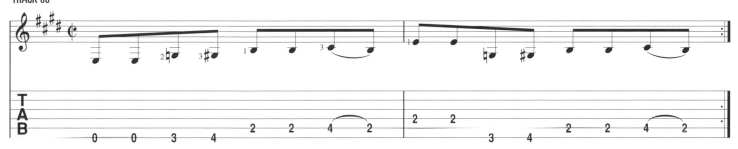

One of the all-time great boogie patterns is Commander Cody's "Hot Rod Lincoln." This can be challenging at first, so practice it slowly until you can play it flawlessly, then gradually speed it up. This is played mostly in second position, but watch for the shift to fourth position during the B chord, and again at the end.

HOT ROD LINCOLN

TRACK 87

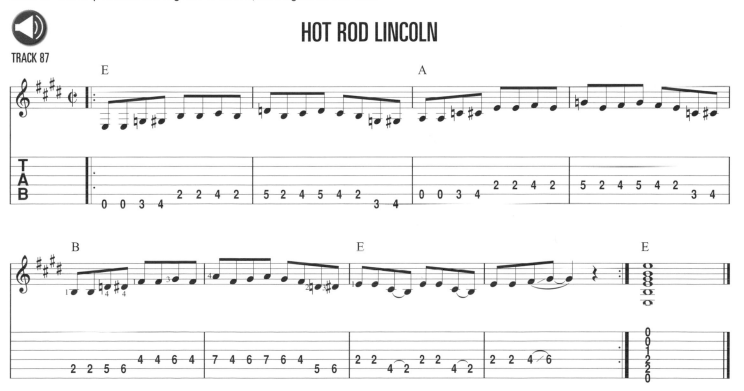

BLENDED LICKS

Here are some licks using the combination of major pentatonic with the added flat 3rd and the blues scale.

SIXTHS

The last lick above ends with intervals of a sixth. Sixths, like thirds, are a popular intervallic tool in country music for licks, fills, etc. They are frequently used in an ascending or descending pattern on the neck of the guitar, usually accenting the chord tones and/or a scale.

Here are three examples of sixth patterns in E, using the first and third strings.

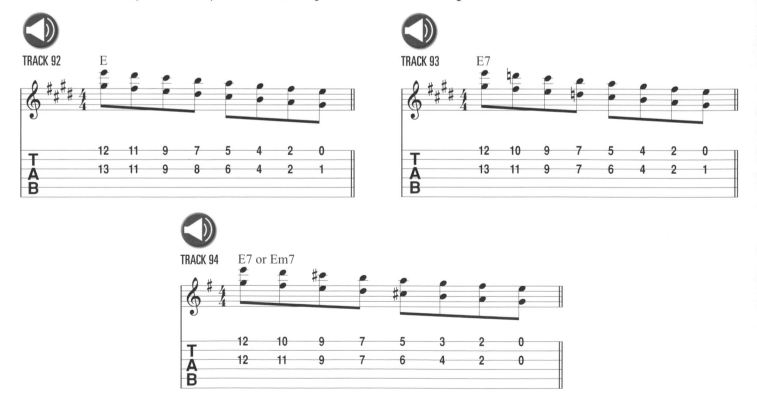

When using sixths over a dominant seventh chord, adding a couple of chromatic passing tones can be particularly effective.

TRACK 95

Here are two more sixth licks for an E7 chord.

TRACK 96
FAST/SLOW

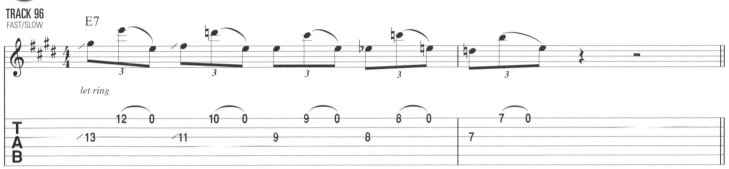

TRACK 97
FAST/SLOW

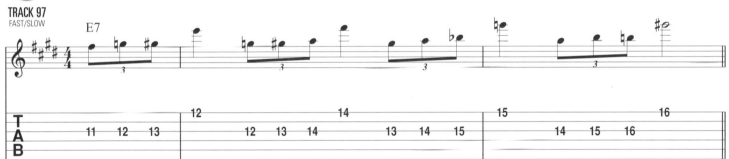

Here's a great pedal steel-type lick using sixths.

TRACK 98
FAST/SLOW

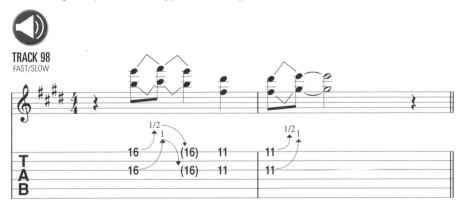

The king of "twang," Duane Eddy, made "Rebel 'Rouser" a country-flavored classic. It is a great tune for us to end on because it incorporates a lot of what we've learned in this book. Play along with the melody, picking close to the bridge to achieve the necessary "twang." Notice that the tune changes keys, or modulates, three times. We start in E, then go to F, then F#, and finally to G. Start in second position for E, move to first position for F and F#, and then finish in second position for G.

REBEL 'ROUSER

TRACK 99

If you like, try soloing over "Rebel 'Rouser." It'll give you one last opportunity to "pick awhile" over, basically, blues chord changes in E, F, F#, and G. Try using the licks you have learned so far as a guide—including the sixths just covered—or try a few of your own. Good luck!

HAL LEONARD GUITAR METHOD

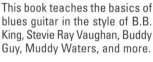

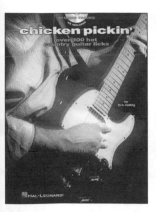
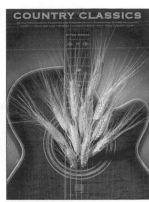

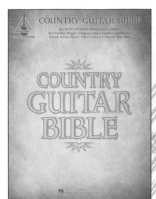
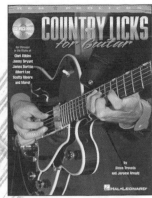
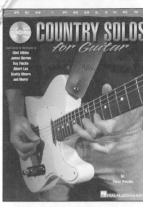
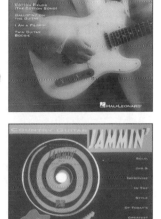

GUITAR PLAY-ALONG

INCLUDES TAB

The Guitar Play-Along Series will help you play your favorite songs quickly and easily. Just follow the tab and listen to the CD to hear how the guitar should sound, and then play along using the separate backing tracks. Mac or PC users can also slow down the tempo by using the CD in their computer. The melody and lyrics are also included in the book in case you want to sing, or to simply help you follow along. 8 songs in each book.

VOLUME 1 – ROCK GUITAR
Day Tripper • Message in a Bottle • Refugee • Shattered • Sunshine of Your Love • Takin' Care of Business • Tush • Walk This Way.
00699570 Book/CD Pack $12.95

VOLUME 2 – ACOUSTIC GUITAR
Angie • Behind Blue Eyes • Best of My Love • Blackbird • Dust in the Wind • Layla • Night Moves • Yesterday.
00699569 Book/CD Pack $12.95

VOLUME 3 – HARD ROCK
Crazy Train • Iron Man • Living After Midnight • Rock You like a Hurricane • Round and Round • Smoke on the Water • Sweet Child O' Mine • You Really Got Me.
00699573 Book/CD Pack $14.95

VOLUME 4 – POP/ROCK
Breakdown • Crazy Little Thing Called Love • Hit Me with Your Best Shot • I Want You to Want Me • Lights • R.O.C.K. in the U.S.A. (A Salute to 60's Rock) • Summer of '69 • What I like About You.
_____00699571 Book/CD Pack $12.95

VOLUME 5 – MODERN ROCK
Aerials • Alive • Bother • Chop Suey! • Control • Last Resort • Take a Look Around (Theme from   "M:I-2") • Wish You Were Here.
_____00699574 Book/CD Pack $12.95

VOLUME 6 – '90S ROCK
Are You Gonna Go My Way • Come Out and Play • I'll Stick Around • Know Your Enemy • Man in the Box • Outshined • Smells like Teen Spirit • Under the Bridge.
_____00699572 Book/CD Pack $12.95

VOLUME 7 – BLUES GUITAR
All Your Love (I Miss Loving) • Born Under a Bad Sign • Crosscut Saw • I'm Tore Down • Pride and Joy • The Sky Is Crying • Sweet Home Chicago • The Thrill Is Gone.
_____00699575 Book/CD Pack $12.95

VOLUME 8 – ROCK
All Right Now • Black Magic Woman • Get Back • Hey Joe • Layla • Love Me Two Times • Won't Get Fooled Again • You Really Got Me.
_____00699585 Book/CD Pack $12.95

VOLUME 9 – PUNK ROCK
All the Small Things • Fat Lip • Flavor of the Weak • Hash Pipe • I Feel So • Pretty Fly (For a White Guy) • Say It Ain't So • Self Esteem.
_____00699576 Book/CD Pack $12.95

VOLUME 10 – ACOUSTIC
Have You Ever Really Loved a Woman? • Here Comes the Sun • The Magic Bus • Norwegian Wood (This Bird Has Flown) • Space Oddity • Spanish Caravan • Tangled up in Blue • Tears in Heaven.
_____00699586 Book/CD Pack $12.95

VOLUME 11 – EARLY ROCK
Fun, Fun, Fun • Hound Dog • Louie, Louie • No Particular Place to Go • Oh, Pretty Woman • Rock Around the Clock • Under the Boardwalk • Wild Thing.
_____00699579 Book/CD Pack $12.95

VOLUME 12 – POP/ROCK
Every Breath You Take • I Wish It Would Rain • Money for Nothing • Rebel, Rebel • Run to You • Ticket to Ride • Wonderful Tonight • You Give Love a Bad Name.
_____00699587 Book/CD Pack $12.95

VOLUME 13 – FOLK ROCK
Leaving on a Jet Plane • Suite: Judy Blue Eyes • Take Me Home, Country Roads • This Land Is   Your Land • Time in a Bottle • Turn! Turn! Turn! (To Everything There Is a Season) • You've Got a Friend • You've Got to Hide Your Love Away.
_____00699581 Book/CD Pack $12.95

VOLUME 14 – BLUES ROCK
Blue on Black • Crossfire • Cross Road Blues (Crossroads) • The House Is Rockin' • La Grange • Move It on Over • Roadhouse Blues • Statesboro Blues.
_____00699582 Book/CD Pack $12.95

VOLUME 15 – R&B
Ain't Too Proud to Beg • Brick House • Get Ready • I Can't Help Myself (Sugar Pie, Honey Bunch) • I Got You (I Feel Good) • I Heard It Through the Grapevine • My Girl • Shining Star.
_____00699583 Book/CD Pack $12.95

VOLUME 16 – JAZZ
All Blues • Black Orpheus • Bluesettc • Footprints • Misty • Satin Doll • Stella by Starlight • Tenor Madness.
_____00699584 Book/CD Pack $12.95

VOLUME 17 – COUNTRY
All My Rowdy Friends Are Coming over Tonight • Amie • Boot Scootin' Boogie • Chattahoochee • Folsom Prison Blues • Friends in Low Places • T-R-O-U-B-L-E • Workin' Man Blues.
_____00699588 Book/CD Pack $12.95

VOLUME 18 – ACOUSTIC ROCK
About a Girl • Breaking the Girl • Drive • Iris • More Than Words • Patience • Silent Lucidity • 3 AM.
_____00699577 Book/CD Pack $12.95

VOLUME 19 – SOUL
Get up (I Feel like Being) a Sex Machine • Green Onions • In the Midnight Hour • Knock on Wood • Mustang Sally • (Sittin' On) the Dock of the Bay • Soul Man • Walkin' the Dog.
_____00699578 Book/CD Pack $12.95

VOLUME 20 – ROCKABILLY
Blue Suede Shoes • Bluejean Bop • Hello Mary Lou • Little Sister • Mystery Train • Rock This Town • Stray Cat Strut • That'll Be the Day.
_____00699580 Book/CD Pack $12.95

Prices, contents, and availability subject to change without notice.

FOR MORE INFORMATION, SEE YOUR LOCAL MUSIC DEALER,
OR WRITE TO:

HAL•LEONARD
CORPORATION
7777 W. BLUEMOUND RD. P.O. BOX 13819 MILWAUKEE, WI 53213

Visit Hal Leonard online at www.halleonard.com